"R" is for Research

Toni Buzzeo

Illustrated by Nicole Wong

UpstartBooks

Fort Atkinson, Wisconsin

"R" is for

Research

By **TONI BUZZEO**

Illustrated By **Nicole Wong**

A is for assignment. We've got research to do.

B is for books.
Some are old;
some brand new.

C is for curiosity.
We have questions in mind.

D is for discovery.
Who knows WHAT we will find?

E is for essential
reference items to use.

F is for facts
   in the sources we'll choose.

GOALS
Cat Research

TOPICS
Breeds
Physical Characteristics
Behavior
Family and Young
History and Mythology

RESOURCES
Reference Books
Nonfiction Books
Newspapers and Magazines
Websites and online articles
Primary Sources

G is for goals.
Decide how to proceed.

H is for highway,
information we need.

I is for Internet,
online places to hunt.

J is for journals
that arrive every month.

K is for knowledge
on the pages we turn.

M is for media center
where we fill up our minds.

N is for note taking,
recording facts that we find.

O is for organize,
    sort and cite facts in turn.

P is for product.
Now we'll show
what we've learned.

Q is for questions
we answered in advance.

R is for research.
It's the seek-and-find dance.

S is for success.
We are nearly there now.

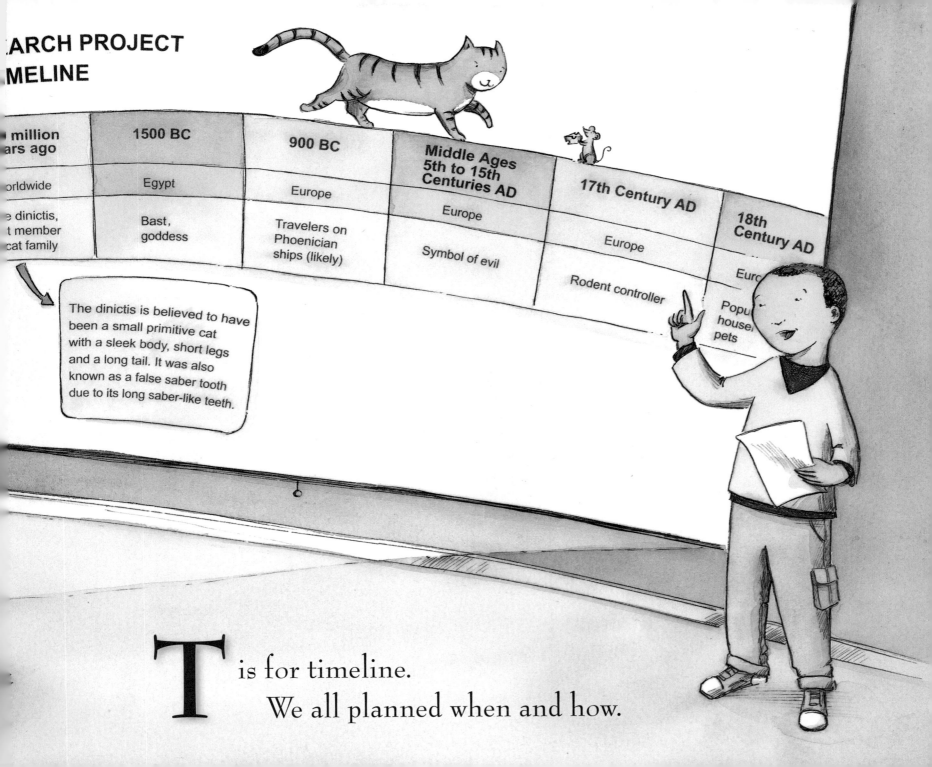

million ars ago	1500 BC	900 BC	Middle Ages 5th to 15th Centuries AD	17th Century AD	18th Century AD
orldwide	Egypt	Europe	Europe	Europe	Eur
e dinictis, t member cat family	Bast, goddess	Travelers on Phoenician ships (likely)	Symbol of evil	Rodent controller	Popu house pets

The dinictis is believed to have been a small primitive cat with a sleek body, short legs and a long tail. It was also known as a false saber tooth due to its long saber-like teeth.

T
is for timeline.
We all planned when and how.

U is for understanding.
It increased as we searched.

W is for website
where we posted results.

X is for eXtra,
one last source to consult.

Y is for yesterday,
long before we knew how.

Z is for ZOWIE!
We're all researchers now!

To Heidi, who can pull a rabbit (or a cat)
out of a hat at a moment's notice.

—T.B.

To my resourceful librarians.

—N.W.

Text © 2008 by Toni Buzzeo
Illustrations © 2008 by Nicole Wong

The paper used in this publication meets the minimum requirements of American
National Standard for Information Science — Permanence of Paper for Printed
Library Material. ANSI/NISO Z39.48.